Zelda Wisdom™

Carol Gardner

Photographs by Shane Young

**Andrews McMeel
Publishing**

Kansas City

03 04 05 CTP 10 9

ISBN: 0-7407-1897-5

Library of Congress Card Catalog Number: 2001090183

Attention: Schools and Businesses

Andrews McMeel books are available at quantity discounts with bulk purchase
for educational, business, or sales promotional use. For information, please write to:
Special Sales Department, Andrews McMeel Publishing, 4520 Main Street,
Kansas City, Missouri 64111.

Acknowledgments

A large cast of characters has helped me achieve my doggy-diva status. I would like to thank, first and foremost, those "in house": Shane Young, my photographer; Sandi Serling, my publicist; Angie Galimanis of Serling & Associates; and Lesly Verduin at Zelda Wisdom, Inc.

Thanks also to the wonderful people at the Beanstalk Group, Portal Publications, and Andrews McMeel. Without my "couture creators," Irene Duffy and Sue Cornell, I would still be running naked through the park. And without my trainer and friend, Cindy Cantlon, I wouldn't know which fork to use or that I shouldn't bite the hand that feeds me. Of course, Jay Gardner, my "brother" of sorts, deserves a big thanks. He taught me how to climb stairs and how to rock and rumble.

I would be remiss if I didn't end by thanking my boyfriend, Chauncey, and my favorite playmates, Daphne and Baby Zelda. Good friends are everything.

—Zelda

The Evolution of Zelda

Here I sit ... a heavy-breathing, short-legged, pudgy chick with bloodshot eyes and more wrinkles than a linen skirt in the summer. But here's the kicker ... people love me.

It all started when I was an ugly little pup. A lonely lady who was going through some tough times adopted me. A friend told her she had two choices, either see a therapist or get a dog. She says it was love at first sight. I figure she took one look at me and thought to herself, "Well, it could be worse." Whatever the case, we went home together.

Home was a ranch. My less-than-short legs were a definite disadvantage for dealing with horses; I just couldn't catch them. Fortunately, the lady liked to take photographs of me. She said I made her laugh because I was a mirror image of what she felt inside.

During the holidays she put me in a bubble bath, made a bubble-beard on my face, and placed a red Santa hat on my head. The photo from that experience turned into our first card. "For Christmas I got a dog for my husband . . . good trade, huh?" Friends loved it and wanted more.

That was the beginning of my fame and future. As the demand for Zelda cards increased, I donned more costumes than a drag queen. From tutus to togas, from boxing gloves to biker leathers . . . I've been there and I love it. I'm spoiled with tummy rubs and caramel ice-cream bars. Limousines drive me to television appearances and universities add honorary "Pet" degrees to my list of accomplishments. With enviable measurements of 32-32-32, they are calling me "the hottest supermodel to come along." Imagine that!

Some people might think I entered the world with a lot of disadvantages. After all, I have jowls that neither cosmetic surgery nor duct tape can repair and an underbite only a snowplow would appreciate. But it's how you look at it. What appears as a disadvantage can be turned into an advantage. If I'm not a good example of that, I don't know what is.

My wisdom? Be happy with who you are and with what you've been given. Be tough, but tender … sweet but strong.

Enjoy life. Grin, it's good.

There is a little of me in all of you.

—Zelda

Got Attitude?

Why BEE normal?

When you're the queen . . .
you can do anything.

I don't suffer from insanity ...
I enjoy every minute of it.

If you can't take the heat,
get out of the kitchen.

Had milk . . . want beer.

Had beer . . . want milk.

I'm a morning person . . . at noon!

Plato and Socrates were just
quoting their mothers.

When the Going Gets Tough

Life is tough . . . wear a helmet.

Grab life by the throttle . . .

and don't look back.

Tough times never last ...
tough people do.

Just about the time
you make ends meet ...
somebody moves the ends.

Life is tough . . .

but I'm tougher.

Beware of "woofs"
in sheep's clothing.

Cowgirls ...how the West was won!

When life sucks ... bite back.

I WILL survive!

Going through hell? Keep going.

It Takes TWO!

1 dog + 3 martinis = 1 FOX

When I'm good, I'm very good ...
when I'm bad, I'm better.

Lead me not into temptation . . .

I can find it myself.

Love me tender.

LOVE must EVOLve.

Don't save love for a rainy day.

Love hurts.

Behind every Zuperman

is a Zuperwoman.

A friend is always there for you.

A good relationSHIP is a lifesaver.

It Figures . . .

Diet? . . . Fuhgedaboudit.

Currently in training . . .
for a midlife crisis.

I get enough exercise
just pushing my luck.

Go braless . . .

it pulls the wrinkles down.

The weather is here ...

wish you were beautiful.

Well . . . so much for the Nordic Track.

Feeling Good

Whatever makes you happy.

Why worry? . . . Be happy.

Smile . . . it could be worse!

Your fortune? . . . Are you sitting down?

Cheer up!

They sent me ...
the other angels were busy.

He who laughs ... lasts.

He who laughs last ... thinks slowest.

Zelda's Wisdom

ENJOY LIFE . . . this is not a rehearsal!

Celebrate!

This is as good as it gets.

There's no good time ...
only lost time.

It's not over ... until the fat lady sings.